RECIPES

Compiled by Julia Skinner

THE FRANCIS FRITH COLLECTION

www.francisfrith.com

First published in the United Kingdom in 2012 by The Francis Frith Collection®

This edition published exclusively for Identity Books in 2012 ISBN 978-1-84589-676-8

Text and Design copyright The Francis Frith Collection®
Photographs copyright The Francis Frith Collection® except where indicated.

The Frith® photographs and the Frith® logo are reproduced under licence from
Heritage Photographic Resources Ltd, the owners of the Frith® archive and trademarks.
'The Francis Frith Collection', 'Francis Frith' and 'Frith' are registered trademarks of
Heritage Photographic Resources Ltd.

British Library Cataloguing in Publication Data

Flavours of Devon - Recipes
Compiled by Julia Skinner

The Francis Frith Collection
Oakley Business Park,
Wylye Road, Dinton,
Wiltshire SP3 5EU
Tel: +44 (0) 1722 716 376
Email: info@francisfrith.co.uk
www.francisfrith.com

Printed and bound in Malaysia
Contains material sourced from responsibly managed forests

Front Cover: **BARNSTAPLE, BUTCHERS ROW 1919** 69323p
Frontispiece: **EXETER, STEPCOTE HILL 1911** 63678x
Contents: **BIGBURY-ON-SEA, LOBSTER CATCHING c1940** B92002

The colour-tinting is for illustrative purposes only, and is not intended to be historically accurate

CONTENTS

RECIPE

LIKKY SOUP

'Likky' is a Devon name for leeks. This hearty soup combines leeks with 'teddy' – the Devon term for potatoes.

3 large leeks
1 onion
3 medium-sized potatoes
1 rasher of streaky bacon
25g/1oz butter
1.2 litres/2 pints chicken stock
A pinch of grated nutmeg
150ml/ ¼ pint cream
Salt and pepper
Fresh chopped parsley to garnish

Wash the leeks thoroughly and chop them, keeping as much of the green part as possible. Peel and slice the onion. Peel the potatoes and chop into small cubes. Remove the rind from the bacon rasher and cut into small pieces. Put the bacon pieces into a large saucepan, and heat until the fat runs. Add the butter, and when it has melted add the leeks and onion. Cook for a few minutes until the vegetables have softened, then add the potato cubes and mix well. Add the stock and a pinch of nutmeg and bring to the boil, then reduce the heat, cover the pan and simmer for 25-30 minutes until the vegetables are soft and cooked. Season with salt and pepper.

This soup can be served as it is, or liquidized in a blender or passed through a sieve if a smoother consistency is preferred. Serve with a swirl of cream and some chopped fresh parsley on top.

CLOVELLY, HIGH STREET 1894 33490c

ONION SELLERS

For many years Plymouth, with its direct ferry service to Brittany, saw French onion sellers in the town every year. This photograph shows two young lads standing by the harbour wall with their strings of onions. With their grimy jackets and trousers, they give every impression of having endured an uncomfortable passage.

PLYMOUTH, ONION SELLERS 1907 59208

RECIPE

ENGLISH ONION SOUP

Onions are famously used to make French onion soup, a thick broth made with lightly caramelised onions. This classic old English version of onion soup is creamier and milder. Serves 4.

    4 large or 6 small onions, peeled and finely chopped
    2 stalks celery, trimmed and chopped into small pieces
    50g/2oz butter
    50g/2oz plain flour
    300ml/ ½ pint milk
    900ml/1½ pints chicken or vegetable stock
    Salt and freshly ground black pepper
    ¼ teaspoonful freshly grated nutmeg
    One bay leaf
    2 tablespoonfuls finely chopped fresh parsley
    4 tablespoonfuls single cream

Melt the butter in a large pan over a medium heat with a tablespoonful of water. Add the chopped onions and celery and cook for about 15 minutes until they are very soft, but do not allow them to brown. Stir in the flour, then gradually mix in the milk, stirring continually until you have a smooth mixture, and then blend in the stock, a little at a time, stirring constantly until you have a smooth, creamy soup. Bring the soup to the boil, stirring occasionally so that nothing sticks to the bottom of the pan, then reduce the heat to low. Add salt and plenty of freshly ground black pepper to taste, the freshly grated nutmeg and the bay leaf, then cover the pan and leave the soup to simmer for 30 minutes. Remove the pan from the heat and allow the soup to cool a little.

Take out the bay leaf and discard, then put the soup in batches through a blender or liquidizer until it is smooth. Return to the cleaned-put pan, add most of the finely chopped fresh parsley and warm through. Serve in individual bowls with a tablespoonful of single cream poured into each serving and with a garnish of the remaining chopped parsley.

RECIPE

COCKLE SOUP

All along the Devon coast you will find wonderful shellfish, such as fine lobsters and the excellent crabs that south Devon is especially famous for, as well as scallops, mussels and cockles. Traditionally cockles were mainly collected by tough and redoubtable cockle-women, who worked in all weather conditions as they searched the cold sands for the tell-tale pair of small holes which betray a cockle's presence just below the surface. The woman in the photograph on the opposite page is searching for cockles at low tide on the shores of the River Exe estuary near Exmouth in south Devon. Cockles are often sold ready cooked and out of their shells, to be eaten cold, splashed with vinegar, with brown bread and butter. Fresh cockles bought in their shells can also be used to make this tasty soup, full of the flavour of the sea.

> 1.2 litres/2 pints measure (about 50) fresh cockles in the shells
> 25g/1oz butter
> 25g/1oz plain flour
> 300ml/ ½ pint milk
> 2 sticks of celery, very finely chopped
> Salt and pepper
> 2 tablespoonfuls finely chopped fresh parsley

Put the cockles in a bowl of lightly salted water for about one hour, to remove the sand. Scrub the shells well, then put them in a large pan and cover with well-salted water. Bring the water gently to the boil, shaking the pan from time to time, and cook the cockles until they have just opened – don't cook them any longer, as this will toughen them. Discard any cockles that do not open. Leave to cool, then strain the cockles, reserving the cooking liquid. Remove the cockles from their shells with the point of a sharp knife. Melt the butter in a pan, stir in the flour, then gradually mix in 600ml (1 pint) of the cockle water and the milk whilst bringing the mixture to the boil, stirring continually, until it has thickened and formed a smooth consistency. Add the celery, reduce the heat and simmer for 30 minutes, then add the shelled cockles, most of the chopped parsley and salt and pepper to taste. Cook for a few minutes longer before serving, garnished with the reserved chopped parsley.

EXMOUTH, A COCKLE WOMAN 1906 53961

7

RECIPE

BAKED JOHN DORY

A popular fish caught from the south Devon fishing port of Brixham is John Dory, often known as St Peter's fish – the black 'thumbprints' on each side of its head are said to be the marks of St Peter, who was a fisherman. Serves 4.

> 4 John Dory fillets, washed and wiped dry
> 225g/8oz prawns
> 50g/2oz button mushrooms
> 1 teaspoonful anchovy essence
> 1 egg, beaten (optional)
> Salt and pepper
> 1 tablespoonful white wine or cider

Pre-heat the oven to 220°C/400°F/Gas Mark 6. Cut the fish into oblong strips. Finely chop the prawns and mushrooms and mix with the anchovy essence. Moisten, if necessary, with a little beaten egg. Put a quarter of this mixture on to each strip of fish and roll them up into little parcels, securing with a wooden cocktail stick if necessary. Put into a buttered ovenproof dish, season with salt and pepper and moisten with the wine or cider. Cover with buttered greaseproof paper and cook in the pre-heated oven for about 15 minutes, depending on the thickness of the fillets.

BRIXHAM, TRAWLERS, WAITING FOR A BREEZE 1889 21556

RECIPE

HAKE BAKED IN CIDER

A lot of hake is caught off the Devon coast, and is available most of the year. A member of the cod family, it is a delicious fish with a firm flesh and flaky texture. It is sold as steaks, cutlets or fillets and may be grilled, fried or poached, but in this recipe it is baked in the oven with three very traditional ingredients in Devonshire cookery – parsley, cream and cider (see page 50). If hake proves hard to find, you can use cod, whiting, pollock or coley in this recipe instead. Serves 4-6.

> 4-6 hake steaks (cutlets), or skinned fillets
> 225g/8oz fresh tomatoes, skinned and sliced
> 50g/2oz mushrooms, sliced
> 1 tablespoonful finely chopped fresh parsley
> Salt and freshly ground pepper
> 150ml/ ¼ pint dry cider
> 2 tablespoonfuls double cream
> 2 tablespoonfuls fresh white breadcrumbs
> 50g/2oz grated hard cheese of choice

Pre-heat the oven to 180ºC/350ºF/Gas Mark 4.

Wipe the fish pieces thoroughly, pat them dry with a paper towel and arrange them in a single layer in a large buttered ovenproof dish. Cover the fish with the sliced tomatoes, mushrooms, and parsley. Season to taste with salt and freshly ground black pepper, and pour the cider over. Cover with the dish with its lid or a tightly-fitted piece of buttered kitchen foil and bake in the pre-heated oven for 25 minutes. Take out the dish from the oven, remove the lid or foil, and gently stir in the double cream. Sprinkle the breadcrumbs and cheese over the dish to make a topping. Place the dish under a pre-heated hot grill and cook until the cheese has melted and the topping is crisp and browned. Serve with sauté or new potatoes and a green vegetable.

RECIPE

TORBAY SOLE WITH LEMON AND CAPER SAUCE

Torbay off the south Devon coast is famous for its sole, which is at its best from July to February. Torbay sole is also known as lemon sole, and witch sole is also caught, similar to lemon sole but thinner. In this recipe, fillets of Torbay sole are served with a zesty dressing that is also good with skate, plaice, brill and Dover sole. Serves 4.

> 4 large or 8 small fillets of Torbay (lemon) sole,
>   with the black skin removed
> 2 tablespoonfuls plain flour
> 25g/1oz butter, melted
> Salt and pepper
> For the dressing:
> Juice of 2 lemons
> 50g/2oz unsalted butter
> 4 teaspoonfuls capers, drained and rinsed
> 1 tablespoonful chopped fresh parsley

Pre-heat the grill to hot. Line a grill pan with kitchen foil and place it under the grill to heat up. Toss the fish fillets in the flour so that all sides are lightly coated, then brush both sides of the fish with the melted butter and season to taste with salt and pepper. Place the fish fillets on the hot foil in the grill pan. Cook under a hot grill for 2-8 minutes depending on the thickness of the fish fillets, without turning them over, until they are golden brown. When cooked, arrange the fish on a hot serving dish, and keep warm whilst you make the dressing.

Add 4 tablespoonfuls of water to the lemon juice. Heat the butter in a heavy-based pan until it is melted and browned, but not scorched. Add the lemon juice, half at first, then taste the sauce and add the other half if you want. Add the capers and parsley, and season well to taste. Pour the dressing over the fish and serve, with vegetables such as new potatoes and peas, green beans or wilted spinach.

RECIPE

STUFFED MACKEREL WITH GOOSEBERRY SAUCE

Mackerel are caught in great numbers all along the Devon coast, and are delicious. In this recipe they are served with a tasty stuffing and a sauce made from gooseberries, which have long been a favourite accompaniment to mackerel in West Country cookery. Gooseberry jam is also very good served as a relish with cold smoked mackerel fillets, together with brown bread and butter. This amount serves 4, so increase the quantities for more people.

> 4 mackerel, gutted and de-scaled
> 1 tablespoonful finely chopped fresh parsley
> 1 tablespoonful finely chopped thyme
> Half a teaspoonful grated lemon rind
> 1 tablespoonful lemon juice
> 25g/1oz soft white breadcrumbs
> Enough seasoned plain flour to coat the fish
> 1 tablespoonful cooking oil
> 225g/8oz gooseberries
> 25g/1oz butter
> 2-4 tablespoons sugar, according to taste

First of all, prepare the gooseberry sauce. Simmer the gooseberries in very little water until they are very soft, then rub them through a sieve, or purée in a blender. Stir in the butter until it melts, and sweeten the sauce lightly with a little sugar, to taste. Set aside until the mackerel are cooked.

Pre-heat the oven to 180°C/350°F/Gas Mark 4. Wash, dry and clean the mackerel. Combine the parsley, thyme, lemon rind, lemon juice and breadcrumbs and stuff the mackerel with the mixture. Roll the fish lightly in seasoned flour to coat them on all sides. Heat the oil in a baking tin and put in the mackerel to lie side by side. Put the tin in the pre-heated oven and bake, uncovered, for 30 minutes, carefully turning the fish over halfway through. When the mackerel are ready, warm the gooseberry sauce through and serve it with the fish.

RECIPE

MARINATED HERRINGS OR MACKEREL

A popular dish in Devon in the past was 'soused' herrings or mackerel, in which the fish are baked in vinegar and spices, and then eaten cold. This allowed a glut of fish to be cooked and preserved, as they could then be kept in a cool place for several days if necessary. This is another West Country way of preparing the fish, by baking them in a marinade made with vinegar and cold tea. Although it may sound odd, it is an excellent way of preparing the fish. It gives them a wonderfully delicate flavour, and makes a delicious first course or light lunch or supper dish. Serves 4-8 people, depending on appetite.

> 8 herrings or mackerel, cleaned and split open
> 8 bay leaves
> 16 whole black peppercorns
> 1 tablespoonful dark brown sugar
> 150ml/ ¼ pint white wine vinegar, or cider vinegar
> 150ml/ ¼ pint cold, milkless tea

Pre-heat the oven to 180°C/350°F/Gas Mark 4. Place a bay leaf inside each fish. Arrange the fish side by side in an ovenproof dish, and sprinkle over the brown sugar and peppercorns. Mix together the vinegar and cold tea and pour over the fish. Cover the dish with foil and bake in the pre-heated oven for 50-60 minutes. Remove from the oven and leave the fish in the dish to get completely cold in the cooking liquor, which will jell as it cools. Serve the fish cold, with some jellied liquor with each portion.

Fresh pilchards are also very good prepared this way – they used to be caught in great numbers by Devon fishermen, with Plymouth being a major centre for south Devon's pilchard fishing industry.

The use of 'Plymouth' as a name originates from the 13th century. Before then the settlement was called Sutton, a name that still survives today for the picturesque harbour area of Plymouth. This photograph shows the Barbican at Sutton Harbour, for many centuries the home of Plymouth's fishing fleet. Plymouth hookers were essentially long liners, varying in size from 25ft to 40ft and from between five and fourteen tons. During the 1880s and 1890s, when this photograph was taken, there were about 200 hookers registered locally. As the hookers rarely spent more than twenty-four hours at sea, much of the town's fresh fish was landed from them. By the time this photograph was taken, a few were working with light trawler gear. The city's fish market was located here until the late 1990s, when it moved across the harbour to a new purpose-built dock. The cobbled streets and granite steps seen in this view remain, but in place of shipping offices and fish salesmen are now ice-cream parlours, cafés and souvenir shops.

PLYMOUTH, THE BARBICAN 1890 22474

The photograph on the previous page shows The Barbican at Plymouth, from where the Elizabethan seaman and adventurer Francis Drake began his historic circumnavigation of the world in the 'Golden Hind' in 1577; no other ship had made such a voyage before. On his return in 1580, Drake was knighted by Queen Elizabeth I. A Devon man (born in Tavistock in 1544), Sir Francis Drake became mayor of Plymouth in 1590. During his mayoralty he oversaw the bringing of a fresh water supply to Plymouth by the construction of Drake's Leat, which brought water 17½ miles from the head of the River Meavy on Dartmoor. In later years an increased supply of fresh water for Plymouth was needed, and Burrator Reservoir was created in 1891. The upper part of Drake's Leat was lost beneath the reservoir, but parts of Drake's Leat are still visible on the moor at Rodborough Down (off the A386) and near Clearbrook. Sir Francis Drake is commemorated in Plymouth with a statue on Plymouth Hoe Promenade, on which a poem celebrates his achievements.

PLYMOUTH, DRAKE'S STATUE 1930 83293

'Great Drake, whose shippe aboute the world's wide wast
In three years did a golden girdle cast.
Who with fresh streames refresht this Towne that first
Though kist with waters, yet did pire for thirst.'

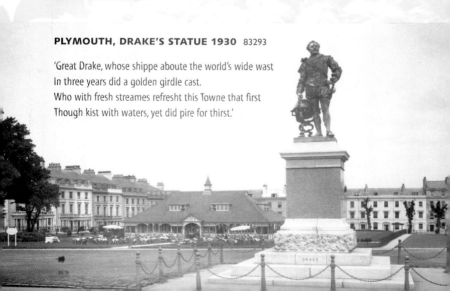

RECIPE

TROUT WITH ALMONDS AND CREAM

For the last 400-plus years the bringing of fresh water to Plymouth by Sir Francis Drake during his mayoralty of the city in 1590-91 has been celebrated by the annual Fishing Feast in June, when the Mayor of Plymouth officially surveys the water supply. The Mayor and his council used to congregate at the head weir of Drake's Leat, but the upper portion of the leat disappeared beneath Burrator Reservoir in the 1890s and the Fishing Feast is now held at the reservoir. During the ceremony, toasts are drunk from a goblet filled with water from the leat: 'To the pious memory of Sir Francis Drake.' Another goblet filled with red wine is then passed round, with each person drinking a further toast: 'May the descendants of him who brought us water never want.' A meal of locally caught trout is eaten, followed by strawberries and cream. Originally the Fishing Feast was a free event, but nowadays tickets have to be purchased. Devon is known for good trout, and this is a favourite way of serving it in English traditional cookery – using Devonshire cream, of course! Serves 4.

> 4 trout, gutted and cleaned
> Plain flour for coating the fish
> Salt and pepper
> 175g/6oz butter
> 50g/2oz blanched almonds
> Juice of half a lemon
> 150ml/ ¼ pint single cream

Mix the flour with salt and pepper and use it to coat the fish on both sides. Melt half the butter in a frying pan. Slide in the trout and cook for about 15 minutes, turning halfway through cooking time, until they are golden brown on both sides and cooked through. Take out the trout from the pan, drain, and keep warm on a serving dish. Clean the pan, then melt the remaining butter in it. Add the almonds and fry them carefully until they are lightly browned. Stir in the lemon juice. Heat the cream gently in a separate pan and pour over the fish. Sprinkle with the almonds and serve.

The River Exe is Devon's main river. It rises in north Devon, on
Exmoor, and flows south for almost 50 miles before reaching the
sea at Exmouth. The men seen fishing with nets in this photograph
of the River Exe at Countess Wear are almost certainly after salmon.
The Exe was formerly one of Devon's richest salmon rivers, although
as early as the 19th century concern was being expressed about the
level of the stocks – vast numbers were taken when they were on
their way upstream to spawn. In 1924 a salmon weighing 64 lbs was
caught in the River Exe by fisherman Richard Voysey. Further west,
excellent salmon is also caught in the River Tamar, which forms
much of the border between Devon and Cornwall.

COUNTESS WEAR, THE BRIDGE OVER THE RIVER EXE 1906 53981

RECIPE

DEVON SALMON IN PASTRY

900g/2 lbs fillet of salmon
Salt and pepper
Lemon juice
1 tablespoonful olive oil
675g/1½ lbs puff pastry
225g/8oz onions or shallots
Half a teaspoonful chopped tarragon
115g/4oz button mushrooms
1 egg, beaten, for glazing the pastry

Oven temperature: 190°C/375°F/Gas Mark 5.

Season the salmon with salt, pepper and lemon juice. Heat the olive oil in a large frying pan and lightly fry the salmon on both sides. Take the salmon out of the pan and leave to cool. Roll out the puff pastry on a floured surface to form an oblong shape large enough to enclose the salmon. Chop the onions or shallots very finely, and sweat them in the pan the fish was cooked in, together with the tarragon. Allow to cool, then spread over one half of the pastry. Thinly slice the mushrooms and place them on top of the onions. Season with salt and pepper. Place the salmon on top of the vegetables, fold over the other half of the pastry to enclose it all, and seal the edges. Place, folded side down, on a well-greased baking sheet and brush the top with beaten egg to glaze. Bake in the pre-heated oven for 1 hour, until the pastry is crisp and golden brown.

Flavours of ...

DEVON

EGG & VEGETABLE DISHES

RECIPE

SCALLOPED EGGS

This was inspired by an old Devon recipe in which single eggs were baked in a scallop shell. It makes a tasty and filling snack or supper dish. This amount is for four servings, best baked in a square or rectangular dish just big enough to hold four broken eggs. If you want to increase the quantities to feed more people, you will need quite a large dish, or several smaller ones.

> 2 rashers bacon
> 15g/ ½ oz cooking or bacon fat, or 1 tablespoonful cooking oil
> 1 medium onion, peeled and finely chopped
> 115g/4oz fresh granary or wholemeal breadcrumbs
> 2 tablespoonfuls finely chopped fresh parsley
> Freshly ground black pepper
> 4 eggs
> 4 tablespoonfuls Devonshire double cream

Pre-heat the oven to 200°C/400°F/Gas Mark 6. Grease a square or rectangular ovenproof dish big enough to hold four broken eggs. Heat the fat or oil in a frying pan. Lightly fry the bacon until the fat runs, then remove it from the pan and chop into very small pieces. Put the chopped onion in the pan and cook until it is soft and transparent. Take the pan off the heat and mix in the breadcrumbs, chopped bacon and parsley, and season to taste with freshly ground black pepper (you should not need to add salt, as the bacon will make the dish salty). Turn the mixture into the greased dish. Make a hollow in the mixture in each of the four corners, and carefully break an egg into each one. Use a spoon or fork to bring up the breadcrumb mixture into a ring around each egg to form a border, so it is sitting in a sort of breadcrumb nest. Spoon one tablespoon of the cream over each egg yolk. Bake in the pre-heated oven until the whites of the eggs are set and the yolks are done to your liking – about 10 minutes for a lightly set egg, about 15-20 minutes for a more firmly set egg. Serve immediately, as the eggs will continue to cook after you take the dish out of the oven.

BIDEFORD, POULTRY
OLD FORD FARM YARD
1890 24806x

RECIPE

LIKKY PIE

This is another recipe using leeks, which were widely grown in Devon gardens in the past, and feature in many traditional Devon recipes. Likky (Leek) Pie was traditionally a dish to serve on high days and holidays.

> 6 medium-sized leeks
> 25g/1oz butter
> 4 rashers of streaky bacon, de-rinded and chopped into small pieces
> Salt and pepper
> 2 eggs
> 150ml/¼ pint double cream, the thickest you can get
> 225g/8oz shortcrust, flaky or puff pastry as preferred

Pre-heat the oven to 200°C/400°F/Gas Mark 6, and grease a deep pie dish, or a flan dish or tin about 20-24cms (8-9 inches) in diameter.

Wash and trim the leeks and chop them into small pieces. Melt the butter in a large frying pan, add the chopped leeks and sweat them over a medium heat for about 15 minutes, until they are soft and tender. Place layers of cooked leeks with bacon pieces in the pie or flan dish, seasoning to taste with a little salt and plenty of pepper as you go, finishing with a layer of leeks.

Beat the eggs with the cream and pour the mixture into the dish over the filling. Stir it in gently, so that it is evenly distributed.

Dampen the edges of the pie dish. Roll out the pastry and fit it over the filling to make a lid, firming the edges down and pinching them to seal them well. Cut two or three crosses in the pastry lid with a sharp knife to allow steam to escape during cooking.

Bake in the pre-heated oven for about half an hour, until the pastry is crisp and golden. This is usually served hot, but it is also nice eaten cold.

Okehampton stands on the road between Exeter and Cornwall on the northern edge of Dartmoor, and must have had some strategic importance in earlier centuries – hence the romantic ruins of its once-grand castle that stand alongside the West Okement river in the town, all that remains of the late Norman castle that was originally erected there in the late 11th century and rebuilt around 1300. However, this picturesque old toll house in Okehampton still exists, and is well maintained. It is no longer thatched – it now sports a smart slate roof.

OKEHAMPTON, THE OLD BUS HOUSE 1906 56053

RECIPE

DEVON LAVER CAKES

The edible purple laver seaweed (more correctly an edible algae) – 'porphyra umbilicalis' – is found all along the coast of north Devon, and has been eaten by local people for centuries. It is best to buy ready prepared laver from a shop, as if you wrench it up from the roots you will kill the plant; professional collectors are careful how they pick it, leaving sufficient on the rocks and stones of the beach to allow the seaweed to grow again. Laver is very nutritious, rich in protein, iron, vitamins and many minerals. When freshly picked it is almost purple in colour, but after it has been rinsed and boiled to make it edible it becomes a dark bright green. The resulting spinach-like mass is how you buy ready-prepared laver. Cooked laver will keep for several days in the fridge. Laver can be used for sauces (laver mixed with some butter and orange juice makes an excellent sauce to go with salmon, mutton, lamb or duck) or for making laver cakes, which are usually enjoyed as a breakfast dish served with bacon, as given here. Serves 4.

> 225g/8oz ready prepared laver
> 50g/2oz fine oatmeal
> 1 teaspoonful lemon juice
> Salt and white pepper
> 8 rashers of back bacon
> 50g/2oz lard or bacon fat for frying

Mix the laver with the oatmeal, lemon juice, salt and plenty of white pepper. Shape the laver mix into pieces about the size of a golf ball and flatten them down slightly to make them into patties. Fry the bacon rashers in the lard or bacon fat, then remove them from the pan and keep them warm. Fry the laver cakes into the hot fat left in the frying pan, for 3-4 minutes on each side, shaping and patting them as they cook. Serve with the cooked bacon.

**EXETER, THE GUILDHALL
1896** 38003

RECIPE

DARTMOUTH PIE (OR DEVON PORK PIE)

6 pork chops, boned, trimmed of fat and cut in half
   if very large
(or 675g/1½ lbs leg of pork, cut into thin slices)
6 medium-sized leeks, trimmed and sliced, or 3 onions,
   peeled and thinly sliced
3 large cooking apples, peeled, cored and cut into slices
2 tablespoonfuls soft brown sugar
Half a teaspoonful freshly grated nutmeg
Half a teaspoonful ground allspice
300ml/ ½ pint dry cider or good stock
225g/8oz shortcrust pastry
Beaten egg or milk to glaze the pastry
Salt and pepper

Pre-heat the oven to 200°C/400°F/Gas Mark 6 and grease a deep pie dish. Place half the meat in the dish, followed by a layer of apples. Sprinkle over half the sugar and spices, then add a layer of leeks or onions. Season well with salt and pepper. Repeat the layers with the remaining ingredients, then pour in the cider or stock. Roll out the pastry to 2cms (¾ inch) larger than the top of the pie dish. Cut a narrow strip from around the pastry, dampen the rim of the dish and fit the strip around it. Brush the strip with water, then lay the pastry lid over the dish, pressing the edges together well to seal them. Brush the lid with beaten egg or milk, and cut two holes in the centre to allow steam to escape. Bake in the pre-heated oven for 20 minutes, then reduce the temperature to 170°C/325°F/ Gas Mark 3, cover the pie with foil, and continue to cook for 1-1¼ hours.

DARTMOUTH, A SHOP IN HIGHER STREET c1875 D7305

RECIPE

SQUAB PIE

*'The squab pye, the herb pye, the leek and pork pye,
on which clouted cream was profusely poured…'*
(From 'Traditions and Recollections', Richard Polwhele, 1816)

Squab Pie was originally made with young pigeons, or 'squabs', but it became more usual to make it with mutton or lamb chops. In past times Devon people served warmed clotted cream with savoury pies like this and the Dartmouth Pie on page 28 (the 'leek and pork pye' of the above quote), but that might be too rich for modern tastes. Serves 4.

> 4 good sized lamb chops, trimmed of excess fat
> 2 onions, peeled and thinly sliced
> 2 large cooking apples, peeled, cored and sliced
> 1 tablespoonful soft brown sugar
> Half a teaspoonful of ground nutmeg
> Half a teaspoonful of ground cinnamon
> 150ml/ ¼ pint dry cider or good stock
> 175g/6oz shortcrust pastry
> Beaten egg or milk to glaze the pastry
> Salt and pepper

Pre-heat the oven to 200°C/400°F/Gas Mark 6. Grease a deep pie dish. Put half the onions and apples in the dish and sprinkle over half the sugar, nutmeg and cinnamon. Lay the lamb chops on top and season with salt and pepper. Cover with the remaining onions and apples, sugar and spices, and season again. Pour in the cider or stock. Roll out the pastry to 2cms (¾ inch) larger than the top of the pie dish. Cut a narrow strip from around the pastry, dampen the rim of the dish and fit the strip around it. Brush the strip with water, then lay the pastry lid over the dish, pressing the edges well to seal them. Brush with beaten egg or milk, and cut two holes in the centre to allow steam to escape. Bake for 20 minutes, then reduce the oven temperature to 170°C/325°F/ Gas Mark 3, cover with foil and continue to cook for 1-1¼ hours.

Flavours of …
DEVON
MEAT

RECIPE

EXMOOR LAMB STEW

4 lamb chops
25g/1oz butter
450g/1 lb small potatoes
115g/4oz mushrooms
50g/2oz button onions or
  shallots
150ml/ ¼ pint stock

4 tablespoonfuls white wine
4 tablespoonfuls cream
Salt and pepper
Fresh herbs, such as parsley,
  thyme, lovage, finely chopped

Melt the butter in a large saucepan. Fry the chops on both sides until browned, remove from the pan and put in the potatoes, mushrooms and onions. Cook for 5 minutes, then remove from the pan. Drain any fat from the pan and add the stock, wine and cream, stirring well to blend it together. Return the chops and vegetables to the pan, add the herbs and season to taste. Cover the pan and simmer the stew gently for about 1 hour, until the chops are tender.

LYNMOUTH, CHERRY BRIDGE 1907 59424

One of the most famous foods associated with Devon is clotted cream. The lush pastures of Devon are grazed by cows whose milk has a high butterfat content, and this has long been a region famous for its butter and cream. The method of preparing clotted cream was a way of preserving it – clotted cream will keep in a cool place for about 2 weeks – and has remained essentially unchanged for over 400 years. It involves heating cream very gently then allowing it to cool, resulting in a thick yellow crust forming which is skimmed off as clotted cream. The time and temperature are crucial, a combination learned by experience. Clotted cream is an essential ingredient of a Devon Cream Tea, and has been enjoyed by visitors to Devon for centuries. It is as popular now as it was when it delighted the 17th-century traveller Celia Fiennes when she visited Devon: 'They scald their cream and milk … and so it is a sort of clouted cream as we call it, with a little sugar, and so put it on top of the apple pie… I was much pleased with my supper.'

(Celia Fiennes, 'Through England on a Side-Saddle 1662-1741'.)

LYNMOUTH, THE TOURIST COACH 1907 59404x

RECIPE

WHORTLEBERRY AND APPLE PIE

Whortleberries are small, dark, edible berries that grow wild on Exmoor and Dartmoor. They are a form of bilberry (Vaccinium myrtillus), and are also known in Devon as worts, hurts or whinberries. They have a delicious flavour and are gathered by local people to make jams, preserves and pies, often teamed with apples, as here, to make a small amount of berries go further. Whortleberries are in season in August and September. They grow on small bushes close to the ground, often hidden under the foliage, and can be hard work to pick, but are worth the effort. However, if you don't want to pick your own whortleberries to make this pie, you can use blackberries or commercially grown blueberries instead.

> 450g/1 lb whortleberries (or alternative fruit – see above)
> 2 cooking apples
> 225g/8oz sugar
> 350g/12oz sweet shortcrust or puff pastry, whichever is preferred
> A little milk and extra sugar, to finish

Heat the oven to 200°C/400°F/Gas Mark 6. Remove the cores from the apples with an apple corer, but do not peel them. Stand the apples in an ovenproof dish, add 2 tablespoonfuls of water to the dish and bake in the pre-heated oven for 40-45 minutes, until the apples are tender. When cooked, scrape out the pulp from the apples and mix it with the bilberries and the sugar. Roll out half the pastry on a lightly floured board and use it to line a greased pie tin about 20cms (8 inches) in diameter. Turn out the fruit mixture into the pie tin. Roll out the remaining pastry to make a lid and place it over the pie, trim and seal the edges and cut two holes in the lid for steam to escape during cooking. Brush the lid of the pie with a little milk to glaze, and sprinkle with sugar. Place in the pre-heated oven and bake for ten minutes, then reduce the heat to 180°/350°C/Gas Mark 4 and cook for a further 30 minutes until the pastry is golden brown and crisp. Serve the pie with custard or a generous helping of Devonshire clotted cream.

RECIPE

APPLE DAPPY

This apple pudding looks rather like a dishful of Chelsea buns, baked in a sticky lemon sauce. This makes a large pudding, enough for 6-8 helpings, so halve the quantities and bake in a smaller dish for 3-4 people. Some people include a handful of raisins as well, sprinkled over the apple filling.

<u>For the lemon syrup:</u>
- 1 large lemon
- 1 tablespoonful golden syrup, or runny honey
- 15g/ ½ oz butter
- 115g/4oz caster sugar
- 200ml/4 fl oz water

<u>For the pudding:</u>
- 225g/8oz self-raising flour
- 1 level teaspoonful baking powder

A pinch of salt
50g/2oz butter, cut into small pieces and softened to room temperature
About 150ml/ ¼ pint milk
450g/1 lb cooking apples
1 tablespoonful demerara or soft brown sugar
Half a teaspoonful ground cinnamon, mixed spice or allspice

TIVERTON, OLD COTTAGES, LITTLE SILVER
1920 69893

34

Pre-heat the oven to 190°C/375°F/Gas Mark 5. Butter a 1.2 litre (2 pint) wide, shallow ovenproof dish (you need something big enough to hold the equivalent of 6 Chelsea buns, side by side).

Make the lemon syrup first. Peel the lemon as thinly as possible, then squeeze out the juice. Place the lemon peel and juice, syrup or honey, butter, caster sugar and water in a saucepan and stir over a gentle heat until the sugar is dissolved. Remove from the heat, set aside and leave the syrup to infuse in the pan whilst you make the pudding.

Sift the flour, baking powder and salt into a large mixing bowl. Rub in the butter with your fingertips until the mixture resembles breadcrumbs. Use a fork or round bladed knife to stir in the milk and form a smooth dough. Gather the dough into a ball and knead it very lightly for a minute or so, until it is smooth and elastic – add a little extra flour if you need to, if the dough is too sticky to work. Turn out the dough onto a lightly floured surface and gently roll it out to about 20cms (8 inches) square and 5mm (¼ inch) thick.

Peel and core the apples, dice them into small pieces and spread them evenly over the dough (add a few raisins now as well, if you want to). Mix together the sugar and spice and sprinkle over the apple pieces. Roll up the dough like a Swiss Roll. Use a sharp knife to cut the dough into 6-8 slices about 2.5cms (1 inch) thick. Arrange the slices flat, cut side down, side by side, in the buttered dish, leaving room between each slice, as they will expand during cooking. If any of the apple mixture comes out of the roll during the slicing process, press it back into the slices in the dish. Strain the syrup through a sieve to remove the lemon rind, then pour the syrup all over the apple slices. Bake in the pre-heated oven for about 30 minutes until the pudding is puffed up, crisp and golden. Serve hot with custard or cream, with some of the lemon sauce left in the dish spooned over each portion.

RECIPE

APPLE DUMPLINGS

Devonians were often nicknamed Devonshire Dumplings in the past because of their love of this dish. Using mincemeat for the filling makes the recipe quick and easy, but if you prefer you can make the filling instead with a mixture of 115g/4oz currants, 4 tablespoonfuls of brown sugar, half a teaspoonful of cinnamon or mixed spice and a little lemon juice. Serves 4.

> 4 large cooking apples
> 4 teaspoonfuls mincemeat
> 4 tablespoons brown sugar
> 25g/1oz butter, cut into 4 pieces
> 16 cloves
> 225g/8oz shortcrust pastry
> A little milk to glaze
> Caster sugar, to finish

Pre-heat the oven to 180°C/350°F/Gas Mark 4.

Core the apples, and peel them. Stuff the core hole in each apple with a teaspoonful of mincemeat topped with a tablespoonful of brown sugar (or the filling, as above), and put a small piece of butter on top of the filling. Press 4 cloves into the outside of each apple.

Roll out the pastry on a lightly floured surface and cut it into 4 rounds, each big enough to enclose an apple – it is helpful to use an upturned side plate as a guide. Sprinkle each circle with a little caster sugar, and set an apple in the centre. Brush the edges of the pastry rounds with a little water, then bring up the pastry over each apple to meet at the top, enclosing it and wrapping it up like a parcel, pressing all the pastry edges together firmly and smoothing them down well to seal them.

Place the dumplings upside down on a greased baking sheet, so the top of the apple where the sealed edges join is at the bottom, to stop them coming undone as they cook. Brush the dumplings with milk and sprinkle with a little caster sugar. Bake in the pre-heated oven for about 30 minutes, until the pastry is crisp and golden and the apples are cooked – test by sticking a skewer into one of the dumplings to make sure the apple is soft. Sprinkle with a little more caster sugar, and serve hot, with custard or cream.

CHAGFORD, MARKET PLACE 1906 56609

RECIPES

PLUM AND WALNUT CRUMBLE

The long estuaries of the rivers of south Devon – which are actually drowned river valleys formed when the sea level rose at the end of the last Ice Age – are very sheltered; as a result they have their own microclimates, which allow market gardening and fruit growing to flourish. Dittisham, on the estuary of the River Dart, was once famous for its plum orchards, particularly for a localised plum variety. The Dittisham Plum, also known as the Dittisham Small Red, only grows around this one village in Devon, and many cottage gardens in the area contain a Dittisham Plum tree. There are many theories about how the plum came to grow there, none of which can be substantiated: one is that the variety originated from a cargo of fruit or seedlings dumped by a ship, which the villagers planted in their gardens; another is that the original trees were brought to the area by nuns from the nearby Priory of Cornworthy; and yet another is that the original plum trees came to the village from Holland or Germany, which may explain why the local name for the plum is the Dittisham Ploughman, a corruption of the German word 'pflaume' for plum.

> 1kg/2 lbs plums, halved and stoned
> 75g/3oz walnut pieces
> 75g/3oz butter or margarine, diced
> 175g/6oz plain flour
> 175g/6oz demerara sugar

Pre-heat the oven to 180°C/350°F/Gas Mark 4 and butter a 1.2 litre (2 pint) ovenproof dish. Spread the walnuts on a baking sheet and place in the oven for 8-10 minutes, until they are evenly coloured. Put the plums into the dish and stir in the nuts and half the sugar. Rub the butter or margarine into the flour, add the remaining sugar and continue to rub in until fine crumbs are formed. Cover the fruit with the crumb mixture and press it down lightly. Bake in the oven for about 45 minutes, until the top is golden brown and the fruit tender. Serve with custard or Devonshire cream.

Junket, or 'curds and cream', was very popular in the past but is not widely eaten now, which is a pity as it is easy to make this fresh, creamy dessert. Junket is made by setting milk with rennet which is not easy to find nowadays, but most Waitrose supermarkets sell Langdale Essence of Rennet, which is used in this recipe and is suitable for vegetarians – look for it near the gelatine, food colourings and flavourings. The Devonshire version of junket is flavoured with brandy and served with clotted cream, making it especially delicious. If you don't want to flavour your junket with brandy, try using the grated zest of 1 orange or lemon. Junket is also delicious made plain with sugar and served with jam, or fresh fruit such as strawberries or raspberries. Junket depends much on the quality of the milk used to make it, which should be whole milk, preferably from a Channel Island breed, which has a high cream content. Single cream can also be used.

  600ml/1 pint whole milk (Channel Island milk is best), or single cream
  1 heaped tablespoonful caster sugar
  2-3 teaspoonfuls brandy (to taste)
  1 dessertspoonful Langdale Essence of Rennet
    (available from Waitrose supermarkets)
  Freshly grated nutmeg, to finish

Put the milk in a pan with the sugar and warm gently to blood heat, 30°C /98°F. (Without a thermometer, this can be judged by putting a finger into the liquid – it should feel neither hot nor cold.) Stir to dissolve the sugar. Remove the pan from the heat and stir in the brandy, then pour the mixture into a nice serving dish and immediately stir in the rennet. Cover the dish and leave aside at room temperature for about 1 hour for the junket to set – do not put the dish in the fridge, or the junket will cool too quickly and won't set. When the junket is set, sprinkle freshly grated nutmeg liberally over the top. The junket can then be kept in the fridge until needed. Serve sprinkled with extra sugar to taste, if necessary, and a helping of cream – it was traditionally served with clotted cream.

Junket was a very popular dish served at seaside villages and country fairs in the past, giving us the phrase 'to go-a-junketing' for an enjoyable day out.

RECIPE

BARNSTAPLE FAIR PEARS

One of the most important fairs in north Devon in the past was the annual Barnstaple Fair in September. Although in modern times it has become mainly a fun fair with rides and sideshows, the chief reason for the fair in earlier centuries was trade, when farmers and merchants from all over the area would bring their beasts and goods to the town for a week of commerce and fun. By the 19th century there was a Cattle Fair Day, when cattle and also sheep were bought and sold, a Horse Fair Day, and a Pleasure Fair Day, when men and women from miles around would come to enjoy themselves. It was a very important event in the annual life of the area. Locally grown pears studded with almonds and stewed in spiced Devon cider used to be a favourite treat sold from stalls at Barnstaple Fair. Nowadays pears are more commonly poached in red wine, which gives them a lovely ruby red colour, but they are also very good done the traditional way, in cider, which gives them a great flavour. This makes a lovely dessert dish, with the poaching liquid made into a delicious syrup to pour over the pears. Choose dessert pears that are perfectly ripe but still firm for this dish – not hard cooking pears. Serves 4.

> 4 large ripe dessert pears, such as Comice pears
> 25g/1oz blanched almonds, split in half
> 75g/3oz caster sugar
> 300ml/ ½ pint cider or red wine, as preferred
> 2 cloves
> Thinly pared rind of half a lemon
> One cinnamon stick, about 8cms (3 inches) long
> 1 heaped teaspoonful of arrowroot

Peel the pears thinly, leaving the stalks on – there is no need to core them. Cut a thin slice from the base of each pear, to give it a flat base to stand on. Spike the pears with the almond halves, 6-8 halves per pear.

Put the sugar, cider or wine, cloves, cinnamon and lemon rind in a saucepan big enough for the pears to fit into snugly. Heat gently until the sugar has dissolved. Stand the pears upright in the pan, and baste with the liquid. Cover the pan and simmer the pears gently until they are tender, basting with the liquid occasionally. This will take 15-30 minutes, depending on how ripe the pears are – test them with a fork, which should go in easily when they are ready. Transfer the pears to a serving dish. Strain the poaching liquid through a sieve, then return it to the pan. Mix the arrowroot with a little cold water until you have a smooth paste, then add this to the saucepan with the liquid. Bring to the boil, stirring until the mixture has thickened slightly, and remove from the heat immediately it reaches boiling point. Pour the syrup over the pears, allow it to cool a little then baste each pear with a further coating. Serve the pears either hot or cold, with thick or clotted Devonshire cream.

BARNSTAPLE, THE STRAND, HORSE FAIR 1923 75164

One of the most famous fairs in the West Country is Widecombe Fair, held at Widecombe in the Moor on Dartmoor on the second Tuesday every September. The fair is commemorated in a famous folk song in which the chorus ends with a long list of people hoping to hitch a lift to the fair on Tom Pearse's grey mare. The final line of the chorus, 'Old Uncle Tom Cobley and all' has given us the phrase that is used as a way of expressing exasperation at the large number of people in a list:

> *Tom Pearse, Tom Pearse, lend me thy grey mare,*
> *All along, down along, out along, lee.*
> *For I want to go to Widecome Fair,*
> *Wi' Bill Brewer, Jan Stewer, Peter Gurney,*
> *Peter Davey, Dan'l Whiddon, Harry Hawk,*
> *Old Uncle Tom Cobley and all,*
> *Old Uncle Tom Cobley and all.*

WIDECOMBE IN THE MOOR, THE VILLAGE SIGN, 1922 73151b

RECIPE

WIDECOMBE FAIR GINGERBREAD BISCUITS

Special sweetmeats, spiced ale and crunchy gingerbread biscuits were traditionally served at Widecombe Fair. The black treacle in this recipe gives these gingerbread biscuits an authentic old-fashioned dark colour and rich flavour, but use golden syrup instead if you prefer. This amount makes 20-24 gingerbread biscuits, depending how large you make them.

        350g/12oz plain flour
        1 teaspoonful bicarbonate of soda
        2 teaspoonfuls ground ginger
        115g/4oz butter or margarine, slightly softened
        175g/6oz soft light brown or caster sugar
        4 level tablespoonfuls (about 60ml) black treacle
          (or golden syrup if preferred)
        1 egg, beaten

Pre-heat the oven to 190°/375°F/Gas Mark 5 and grease two baking trays.

Melt the treacle or syrup in a pan over a gentle heat until it is runny. Remove from the heat and leave to cool a little. Sift the flour, bicarbonate of soda and ground ginger into a mixing bowl. Rub in the butter or margarine until the mixture resembles fine breadcrumbs, then stir in the sugar. Beat the cooled syrup into the beaten egg, then stir into the flour mixture. Mix it together well to form a smooth but quite stiff dough. Flour your hands and roll small pieces of dough between your palms, to form small balls of dough about the size of a golf ball. Place the balls on the baking trays, well spaced out to allow them room to spread whilst cooking without touching each other – you may need to bake the biscuits in several batches. Bake in the pre-heated oven for 12-15 minutes, until they are risen and golden brown. Be careful not to overcook them – they should not be too hard, or too browned. Leave the biscuits on the baking trays to cool for a few minutes, then transfer to a wire rack to cool completely. Store in an airtight container.

RECIPE

SAFFRON CAKE

Saffron is derived from the dried and powdered stigmas of the styles of the saffron crocus. It is one of the most expensive spices, as it requires many thousands of crocus flowers to make a small quantity of saffron. It has long been a popular flavouring in both Devon and Cornwall, giving cakes or loaves a golden colour and a delicious honey-like taste. Saffron cakes or buns were once traditionally only made at Easter.

> A good pinch of saffron threads
> 450g/1 lb strong plain flour
> ½ a teaspoonful salt
> 50g/2oz lard
> 50g/2oz butter or margarine
> 2 teaspoonfuls of fast acting dried yeast
> 75g/3oz caster sugar
> 115g/4oz currants, raisins or sultanas
> (or a mixture, if preferred)
> 150ml/ ¼ pint milk
> 1 egg, beaten, to glaze

Cut the saffron threads into small pieces into a bowl, and add 150ml/ ¼ pint boiling water. Cover, and leave for at least 1-2 hours – or overnight if possible – for the colour and flavour to develop. Sift the flour and salt into a mixing bowl. Cut the lard and butter or margarine into small pieces and rub them into the flour until the mixture resembles fine breadcrumbs. Add the yeast, sugar, and dried fruit and stir it so that it is all well mixed. Make a well in the centre of the mixture. Add the milk to the saffron and water mixture, and gently warm until it is lukewarm. Pour it into the flour mixture and mix it all together. Lightly flour your hands and knead the mixture gently until it can be gathered into a ball of dough.

Cover the bowl with a damp cloth or a piece of oiled cling film, or place the bowl inside an oiled polythene bag, and leave in a warm place to rise, for about one hour.

Grease a 900g/2 lb loaf tin and line it with baking paper. Turn out the dough on to a lightly floured surface and knead it gently for a short time, then place the dough in the prepared loaf tin. Cover again, and leave to rise again for a further 30 minutes.

Pre-heat the oven to 200°C/400°F/Gas Mark 6. Brush the top of the loaf with the beaten egg. Bake the loaf in the pre-heated oven for 40-45 minutes, until it is risen and cooked through (cover the top with foil if the surface is starting to brown too much). Leave in the tin to settle for 15 minutes before turning out on to a wire rack to cool. Store in an airtight container and serve sliced, spread with butter. This also makes excellent toast.

TAVISTOCK, DUKE STREET 1922 73203

RECIPE

HONITON APPLE CAKE

This delicious apple cake recipe from Honiton in east Devon is made with fresh breadcrumbs instead of flour, and is a good way of using up any leftover or stale bread. It has a dense, moist texture, and is like an apple bread pudding. Eat it cold like a cake, or hot as a pudding, with cream or custard.

> 450g/1 lb firm cooking apples
> 1 tablespoonful water
> 1 teaspoonful ground cinnamon
> 115g/4oz dark brown sugar
> 115g/4oz fresh breadcrumbs (either white or brown work well)
> Finely grated zest of one lemon
> 2 eggs, separated
> 115g/4oz butter
> 50g/2oz currants
> 40g/1½ oz cornflour
> Caster sugar to finish

Peel and core the apples, and cut them into chunks. Put the apples in a saucepan with the water, cinnamon and sugar, bring to the boil, then cover and simmer gently over a low heat for 20-30 minutes until the apples are really soft. Push the apples through a sieve, or process them with a blender, to make a smooth apple purée.

Pre-heat the oven to 180°C/350°F/Gas Mark 4. Grease and line a cake or baking tin about 20cms (8 inches) round or square. Melt the butter in a pan over a low heat, then put aside to cool for a few minutes. Beat the egg yolks in a bowl, then add the currants, apple purée and lemon rind. Last of all, beat in the melted butter. Whip the egg whites in a large bowl until stiff. Sift the cornflour on top of the egg whites and use a large metal spoon to fold it in, then gently mix in the breadcrumbs and apple purée mixture. Spoon the mixture into the prepared tin and bake in the pre-heated oven for around 40-45 minutes, until the surface is risen and firm to the touch. Leave to cool in the tin, then turn out and dredge the top generously with caster sugar.

East Devon used to be famous for its lace industry, of which Honiton was the centre. It was a cottage industry, with lace-makers working from home. The main characteristic of Honiton lace is the 'sprigs', design of flowers, leaves or other natural subjects, which are made separately and then sewn onto net to form the finished piece of lace. Honiton lace was high quality, and much in demand in the past. One admirer was Queen Victoria, who ordered it for the flounce for her wedding dress in 1840. Honiton lace was also used to trim the christening gown for her first child in 1841, and that gown was used for the christenings of over 70 subsequent Royal children up to the christening of Lady Louise, daughter of the Earl and Countess of Wessex, in 2004. The gown was then thought too old and precious to be used any more, and a replica gown was made for future Royal christenings. Devon's hand-made lace industry declined in the 19th century after the invention of lace-making machines allowed lace to be made more quickly and cheaply. Allhallow's Museum in Honiton contains a fine collection of Honiton lace, and volunteers demonstrate the craft of Honiton lace-making there in the summer season.

HONITON, LACE MAKER AND LACE c1900 47861b

HONITON LACE MAKER & LACE

RECIPE

DEVONSHIRE SPLITS

These delicious soft yeasted buns are like sweet, fluffy bread rolls and are the traditional alternative to scones in a Devon cream tea, served split open and spread with clotted cream and jam. They are well worth taking the time to make. If served with clotted cream and black treacle they are known as 'Thunder and Lightning'. This quantity makes 12 to 16 splits, depending on how large you want them to be. Like scones, they are best eaten on the same day they are made.

> 15g/ ½ oz fresh yeast, or 2 heaped teaspoonfuls
> (or one 7g sachet) dried bread-making yeast
> 50g/2oz caster sugar
> 150ml/5 fl oz/ ¼ pint warm water
> 75g/3oz butter or margarine
> 150ml/5fl oz/ ¼ pint milk
> 450g/1 lb plain flour
> Pinch of salt
> Icing sugar to finish
> Clotted cream and jam to serve

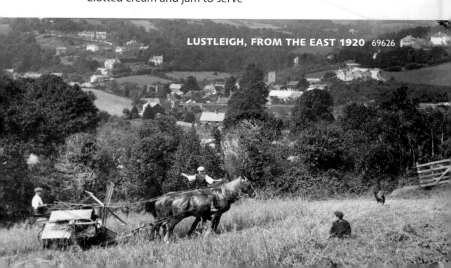

LUSTLEIGH, FROM THE EAST 1920 69626

Sprinkle the yeast and one teaspoonful of the sugar over the warm water in a small bowl or jug, whisk with a fork until the yeast is dissolved, and leave in a warm place for about 10 minutes, until it is activated and frothy.

Whilst the yeast is 'working', put the butter or margarine, milk and remaining sugar into a pan and heat gently until the fat has melted, but do not allow it to boil. Remove from heat and allow it to cool.

Sift the flour and salt into a warmed bowl, make a well in the centre and pour in the yeast and milk mixtures, then mix well to form a soft dough. Leave it to rest for 5 minutes, then turn out onto a floured surface and knead gently for a few minutes, until the dough is smooth and elastic – sprinkle it with a little extra flour if it is still too sticky to work easily. Put the dough back in the bowl, cover with a dampened cloth or put the bowl inside a plastic bag, and leave in a warm place for 1 hour for the dough to rise and double in size. Turn out the dough, knock back and knead again briefly, then shape it into 12-16 small balls, depending on how large you want your splits to be. Place them on a greased baking sheet a little apart, cover with a damp cloth or put in a plastic bag and leave to rise again for about 30 minutes, until they have spread and are just touching.

Bake in a pre-heated oven (200°C/400°F/ Gas Mark 6) for 12-15 minutes, until they are well risen but not over-browned – when cooked, they should still be soft but should sound hollow when tapped. Allow to cool on a wire rack. Dust with icing sugar, and serve split open, cut diagonally from the top across to the bottom, spread with clotted cream and jam. If you are not serving the splits straight away, wrap them in a cloth to keep them soft.

DEVON CIDER

Think of the West Country, and most people associate this area with cider. In his 'View of Devonshire' written in 1630, Thomas Westcote mentions the abundance of Devon orchards, particularly for the making of cider which he describes as 'a drink both pleasant and healthy, much desired of seamen for long southern voyages as more fit to make beverage than beer, and much cheaper and easier to be had than wine'. The secret of making good traditional cider is in the skilled blending of juice from several varieties of cider apples, many of which go by delightful names such as Slack-ma-girdle, Honey String, Buttery Door, and Poor Man's Profit.

Cider was a popular drink in the past, both at home and abroad; by 1820 11,265 hogsheads (each holding 63 gallons) of cider were shipped out from the ports of Exeter and Dartmouth alone. Cider drinking was widely supposed to promote longevity, and John Huxham in 1738 thought the good health of many people in Devon could be attributed to the popularity of the drink. Cider features in many traditional Devon recipes.

In most cider-making counties of England in the past, including Devon, a traditional ceremony known as 'wassailing' was held every year (from the Anglo-Saxon words 'Waes Hal', meaning 'good health'). Wassailing took place in the winter, sometimes on Christmas Eve but usually on Twelfth Night (January 6th). Jugs of cider were carried into the orchards, most of which was drunk, and the rest was poured around the roots of the apple trees whilst a traditional wassailing song was sung. Much noise would be made with banging of pots and pans, to drive away evil spirits and wake up the apple trees for the spring, and sometimes shotguns were fired through the branches. Special cakes would often be eaten, and pieces of cake or bread, soaked in cider, were placed in the trees as a thanksgiving to the tree spirit, and to ensure a good apple crop in the following year.

RECIPE

CIDER CAKE

225g/8oz mixed sultanas, raisins and currants
150ml/5 fl oz/ ¼ pint cider
175g/6oz butter or margarine, softened to room
    temperature
175g/6oz soft brown sugar
3 eggs, beaten
225g/8oz self-raising flour (either plain or wholemeal
    SR flour works well)
1 teaspoonful mixed spice

Soak the dried fruit in the cider overnight, or at least 12 hours before making the cake.

Pre-heat the oven to 180°C/350°C/Gas Mark 4. Grease a 20-24cms (8-9 inches) round or square cake tin and line it with greaseproof paper. Cream the butter or margarine, add the sugar and cream until light and fluffy. Lightly beat the eggs and gradually beat them into the mixture, a little at a time, adding a spoonful of flour to prevent curdling. Stir in the soaked dried fruit and remaining cider. Add the flour and mixed spice, mix thoroughly and beat well. Pour the mixture into the prepared tin and bake just below the centre of the pre-heated oven for about 1 hour and 10 minutes, until the surface is risen and firm to the touch, and a skewer inserted into the middle comes out clean – cover the top with a piece of kitchen foil or greaseproof paper if it seems to be browning too quickly. Leave to settle in the tin for 5 minutes, then turn out onto a wire rack to cool completely.

Old apple tree, we wassail thee, and hoping thou wilt bear
Hat-fulls, cap-fulls, three-bushel bagfuls
And a little heap under the stairs –
Hip! Hip! Hooray!

Flavours of ...

DEVON

TEATIME & BAKING

CHUDLEIGH KNIGHTON
THE CLAY CUTTERS ARMS 1907 58501

FRANCIS FRITH

PIONEER VICTORIAN PHOTOGRAPHER

Francis Frith, founder of the world-famous photographic archive, was a complex and multi-talented man. A devout Quaker and a highly successful Victorian businessman, he was philosophical by nature and pioneering in outlook. By 1855 he had already established a wholesale grocery business in Liverpool, and sold it for the astonishing sum of £200,000, which is the equivalent today of over £15,000,000. Now in his thirties, and captivated by the new science of photography, Frith set out on a series of pioneering journeys up the Nile and to the Near East.

INTRIGUE AND EXPLORATION

He was the first photographer to venture beyond the sixth cataract of the Nile. Africa was still the mysterious 'Dark Continent', and Stanley and Livingstone's historic meeting was a decade into the future. The conditions for picture taking confound belief. He laboured for hours in his wicker dark-room in the sweltering heat of the desert, while the volatile chemicals fizzed dangerously in their trays. Back in London he exhibited his photographs and was 'rapturously cheered' by members of the Royal Society. His reputation as a photographer was made overnight.

VENTURE OF A LIFE-TIME

By the 1870s the railways had threaded their way across the country, and Bank Holidays and half-day Saturdays had been made obligatory by Act of Parliament. All of a sudden the working man and his family were able to enjoy days out, take holidays, and see a little more of the world.

With typical business acumen, Francis Frith foresaw that these new tourists would enjoy having souvenirs to commemorate their days out. For the next thirty years he travelled the country by train and by pony and trap, producing fine photographs of seaside resorts and beauty spots that were keenly bought by millions of Victorians. These prints were painstakingly pasted into family albums and pored over during the dark nights of winter, rekindling precious memories of summer excursions. Frith's studio was soon supplying retail shops all over the country, and by 1890 F Frith & Co had become the greatest specialist photographic publishing company in the world, with over 2,000 sales outlets, and pioneered the picture postcard.

FRANCIS FRITH'S LEGACY

Francis Frith had died in 1898 at his villa in Cannes, his great project still growing. By 1970 the archive he created contained over a third of a million pictures showing 7,000 British towns and villages.

Frith's legacy to us today is of immense significance and value, for the magnificent archive of evocative photographs he created provides a unique record of change in the cities, towns and villages throughout Britain over a century and more. Frith and his fellow studio photographers revisited locations many times down the years to update their views, compiling for us an enthralling and colourful pageant of British life and character.

We are fortunate that Frith was dedicated to recording the minutiae of everyday life. For it is this sheer wealth of visual data, the painstaking chronicle of changes in dress, transport, street layouts, buildings, housing and landscape that captivates us so much today, offering us a powerful link with the past and with the lives of our ancestors.

Computers have now made it possible for Frith's many thousands of images to be accessed almost instantly. The archive offers every one of us an opportunity to examine the places where we and our families have lived and worked down the years. Its images, depicting our shared past, are now bringing pleasure and enlightenment to millions around the world a century and more after his death.

For further information visit: www.francisfrith.com

INTERIOR DECORATION

Frith's photographs can be seen framed and as giant wall murals in thousands of pubs, restaurants, hotels, banks, retail stores and other public buildings throughout Britain. These provide interesting and attractive décor, generating strong local interest and acting as a powerful reminder of gentler days in our increasingly busy and frenetic world.

FRITH PRODUCTS

All Frith photographs are available as prints and posters in a variety of different sizes and styles. In the UK we also offer a range of other gift and stationery products illustrated with Frith photographs, although many of these are not available for delivery outside the UK – see our web site for more information on the products available for delivery in your country.

THE INTERNET

Over 100,000 photographs of Britain can be viewed and purchased on the Frith web site. The web site also includes memories and reminiscences contributed by our customers, who have personal knowledge of localities and of the people and properties depicted in Frith photographs. If you wish to learn more about a specific town or village you may find these reminiscences fascinating to browse. Why not add your own comments if you think they would be of interest to others? See **www.francisfrith.com**

PLEASE HELP US BRING FRITH'S PHOTOGRAPHS TO LIFE

Our authors do their best to recount the history of the places they write about. They give insights into how particular towns and villages developed, they describe the architecture of streets and buildings, and they discuss the lives of famous people who lived there. But however knowledgeable our authors are, the story they tell is necessarily incomplete.

Frith's photographs are so much more than plain historical documents. They are living proofs of the flow of human life down the generations. They show real people at real moments in history; and each of those people is the son or daughter of someone, the brother or sister, aunt or uncle, grandfather or grandmother of someone else. All of them lived, worked and played in the streets depicted in Frith's photographs.

We would be grateful if you would give us your insights into the places shown in our photographs: the streets and buildings, the shops, businesses and industries. Post your memories of life in those streets on the Frith website: what it was like growing up there, who ran the local shop and what shopping was like years ago; if your workplace is shown tell us about your working day and what the building is used for now. Read other visitors' memories and reconnect with your shared local history and heritage. With your help more and more Frith photographs can be brought to life, and vital memories preserved for posterity, and for the benefit of historians in the future.

Wherever possible, we will try to include some of your comments in future editions of our books. Moreover, if you spot errors in dates, titles or other facts, please let us know, because our archive records are not always completely accurate—they rely on 140 years of human endeavour and hand-compiled records. You can email us using the contact form on the website.

Thank you!

For further information, trade, or author enquiries
please contact us at the address below:

**The Francis Frith Collection, Oakley Business Park,
Wylye Road, Dinton, Wiltshire SP3 5EU England.**
Tel: +44 (0)1722 716 376 Fax: +44 (0)1722 716 881
e-mail: sales@francisfrith.co.uk **www.francisfrith.com**